A Tune A Day
FOR TRUMPET OR CORNET.
BY C. PAUL HERFURTH.

BOOK ONE.

Exclusive Distributors:
Music Sales Limited
14-15 Berners Street, London W1T 3LJ, UK.
Music Sales Pty Limited
20 Resolution Drive, Caringbah, NSW 2229, Australia.

Order No. BM10264
ISBN 0.7119.1584.9

THE BOSTON MUSIC COMPANY

DISTRIBUTED BY

HAL•LEONARD®
CORPORATION
7777 W. BLUEMOUND RD. P.O. BOX 13819 MILWAUKEE, WI 53213

FOREWORD TO TEACHERS

IN compiling this course the objective has intentionally been not to cover too much ground; but rather to concentrate on the acquisition of a thorough musical background and solid foundation in good Trumpet and Cornet playing. These two requisites are inseparable.

A brief section is devoted to the simpler rudiments of music which should be thoroughly understood as the need arises.

The learning of new fingerings as introduced should be insisted upon.

Cultivate in the pupil the habit of careful listening.

The familiar hymns and folk-songs have been selected because of their melodic interest as pieces, and because, in addition, in each appears some technical point to be mastered.

The value of learning to " think count" from the very beginning cannot be over-estimated. Only in this way can a pupil sense rhythm. Rhythm, one of the most essential elements of music, and usually conspicuous by its absence in amateur ensemble playing, is emphasized throughout.

Many teachers do the thinking for their pupils, instead of helping them to think for themselves. Insisting upon the mastery of each point will not dull their interest. What greater gratification can there be for a pupil, whether child or adult, than self-accomplishment in a set task?

Lessons marked, "Supplementary Material" may be given as a reward for well-prepared work.

Class teaching should be a combination of individual instruction and ensemble playing. At every lesson there should be individual playing so that all the necessary corrections can be made. Never allow pupils' mistakes to go unnoticed, since only by immediate correction will they develop the habit of careful thinking and playing.

A decided advantage of group-teaching is that it provides experience in ensemble playing and gives every pupil the opportunity of listening to the others, of observing their mistakes, and of profiting from the corrections.

For the best results each class should not be made up of more than six for a half-hour lesson, and twelve for an hour lesson. Irrespective of the numbers, the teacher must see to it that there is individual instruction as well as general class direction.

Classes should be regraded whenever necessary so as not to retard the progress of the more gifted students, or discourage the less musically endowed. This procedure also acts as an incentive for greater effort on the part of the pupils.

The lip slurs on page 31 should be used whenever necessary according to the individual student's requirements.

The tests, following each five lessons, are given as a definite check on the pupil's progress of knowledge and accomplishment. These tests are most important and should not be omitted.

Eventual success in mastering the instrument depends on regular and careful application to its technical demands. Daily practice should not extend beyond the limits of the player's physical endurance—the aim should be the gradual development of lip and breath control alongside assured finger-work.

C. PAUL HERFURTH
Director of Instrumental Music
East Orange, N. J.

RUDIMENTS OF MUSIC

Music is represented on paper by a combination of characters and signs, all of which it is necessary to learn in order to play the Trumpet or Cornet intelligently.

Symbols called notes are written upon and between five lines which is the staff.

The sign placed at the beginning of the staff is called the treble or G clef.

The staff is divided by barlines into bars as follows:

These bars, in turn, are equal in time value, according to the fractional numbers, (Time signature) placed at the beginning of the music.

The time signature indicates the number of notes of equal value in each bar. The upper figure gives the number of beats or counts in a bar, and the lower figure indicates what kind of a note has one beat, such as $\frac{4}{4}$ or **C** equals

four crotchets or the equivalent minim and two crotchets in each bar;

$\frac{2}{4}$ equals 2 crotchets; $\frac{4}{8}$ equals 4 quavers, etc.

There are different kinds of notes, each variety representing a certain time value as follows:

Semibreve equals: Two Minims, Four Crotchets, or Eight Quavers.

The count for the above would be, four to the semibreves; two to each minim; one to each crotchet and one to each group of two quavers.

The notes are named after the first seven letters of the alphabet, i.e., (a, b, c, d, e, f, g,) according to the line on, or space in which they are placed.

The Treble (G) clef which encircles the second line, establishes the note G on this line, from which

the other lines and spaces are named as follows:

G A B C D E F G G F E D

In addition notes are written upon and between short lines above and below the staff. These lines are called leger lines.

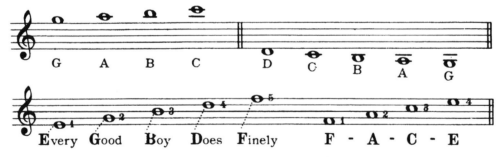

G A B C D C B A G

Every Good Boy Does Finely   F - A - C - E

A rest indicates a pause, or silence for the value of the note after which it is named, such as

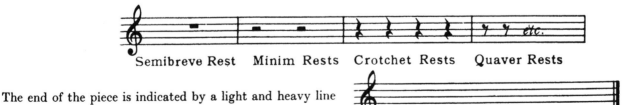

Semibreve Rest   Minim Rests   Crotchet Rests   Quaver Rests

The end of the piece is indicated by a light and heavy line

When a section or part of a piece is to be repeated it will be shown by a double bar with two dots.

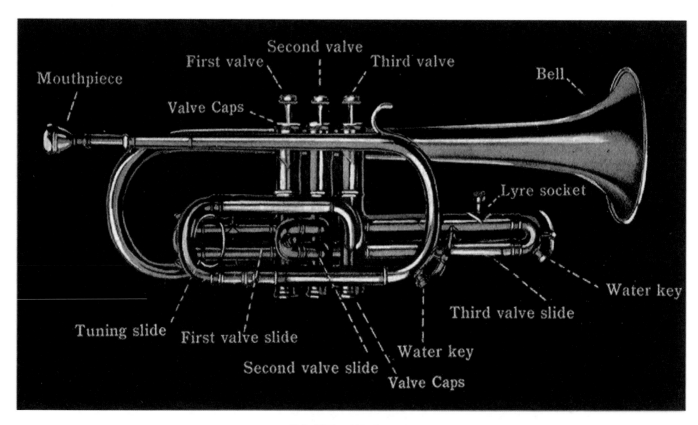

First valve, Second valve, Third valve, Bell, Mouthpiece, Valve Caps, Lyre socket, Water key, Tuning slide, First valve slide, Second valve slide, Water key, Valve Caps, Third valve slide

TO THE STUDENT

A clearer understanding of the construction and mechanics of the instrument you are about to play will prove most helpful in learning your fingering.

When the open notes (no valves) are sounded the shortest length of tubing is in use. By depressing the valves separately or in combination, additional tubing is opened thereby lowering the pitch as follows:

The 2nd. valve lowers the pitch of an open note by ONE-HALF STEP OR SEMITONE.
The 1st.　　,,　　,,　　,, ,, ,, ,, ,,　　,, ,, ONE WHOLE STEP OR TONE.
The 3rd.　　,,　　,,　　,, ,, ,, ,, ,,　　,, ,, ONE TONE AND A SEMITONE
The 2nd. & 3rd. valves lowers the pitch of an open note by TWO WHOLE STEPS OR TONES.
The 1st. & 3rd.　　,,　　,,　　,, ,, ,, ,, ,,　　,, ,, TWO TONES AND A SEMITONE.
All three　　　　,,　　,,　　,, ,, ,, ,, ,,　　,, ,, THREE WHOLE TONES.

From the above it is easy to see that the 1st. & 2nd. valves combined is equal to the 3rd. valve. This 3rd valve however, is rarely used separately except in very rapid playing, as it is slightly out of tune.

TUNING YOUR INSTRUMENT

Cornets and trumpets are pitched in B♭, which means that when you read and finger C, the actual pitch sounding is B♭, thus the piano must play one whole tone lower than the note you are fingering.

PHRASING

The breath marks ('), in addition to indicating the proper places to breathe, also serve as an introduction to the feeling of proper phrasing of melodies. This is important as it is that which gives meaning to music.

FOREWORD TO STUDENTS

PHYSICAL PREPARATION

Mouthpiece front view.　　　　　　　　　　　　　　　　　　*Mouthpiece side view.*

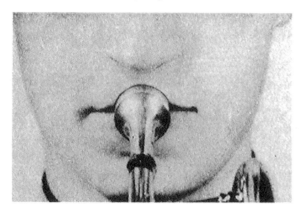
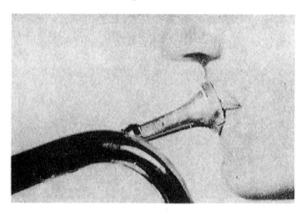

Various ways may be used to help the beginning student produce his first note. The following is one method that has proved successful.

Close the lips and then gradually pull back the corners of the mouth until the lip surfaces are even. (Do not stretch the lips tightly). Take a breath, and, gently blowing, produce a " buzzing " sound. The lips must vibrate in the very centre while producing the " buzz ". When you are able to " buzz " steadily you are ready to place the mouthpiece to the lips.

It is considered good practice to place the mouthpiece half on the upper lip and half on the lower lip in the centre of the mouth. (See pictures). An abnormal mouth formation or tooth structure may necessitate modifications of the above, but in general, it is good to strive to form the embouchure as close as possible like the above.

The tip of the tongue is placed behind the upper teeth, and when ready to produce a **note**, jerk the tongue downwards by using the syllable " TU ". The tongue must be moved very quickly. Breath should be taken through the corners of the mouth. DO NOT PUFF OUT YOUR CHEEKS. Practise in front of a mirror.

CORRECT POSITION (POSTURE)

When playing a trumpet or cornet always stand or sit erect with the head up. The instrument should be held as nearly horizontal as possible, with the arms slightly away from the body. (Fig. 1.)

When practising, it is better to play in a standing position as this will help you to breathe properly.

FINGERING THE VALVES

The first three fingers of the right hand are used to press down the valves. The first finger for the 1st. valve (nearest the mouthpiece) marked (1), the second finger, 2nd valve marked (2), the third finger, 3rd valve marked (3). The fourth or little finger should be free to move with the other fingers. The mark (o) indicates an open note and is played without the use of any valves.

TECHNICAL

The most important tec e
as follows :
(1) Developing and stren
(*Process*) Playing of
(2) Developing clarity ar
(*Process*) Proper use
(3) Developing a fine qu;
(*Process*) A combina
(4) Developing fluency ir
(*Process*) Playing of
(5) Developing a mastery
(*Process*) A combine

Fig. I

CARE OF THE INSTRUMENT

Your cornet (trumpet) will not sound its best, nor will your learning to play it be as easy unless everything pertaining to the instrument is kept in perfect condition.

VALVES: A clean valve will never stick. Lubricate them with a good grade of valve oil. Occasionally clean the valves with a little paraffin or petrol, removing them one at a time. Dry them thoroughly and use fresh oil. Remove, clean and replace one valve at a time.

TUNING AND VALVE SLIDES: These slides, as well as the valve caps, should be greased with a little vaseline to keep them free. Try them twice a week.

MOUTHPIECE AND TUBING: Unless you clean the inside of your instrument, a coating of saliva will form which will greatly interfere with its playing qualities. At least once a week run lukewarm soap suds through your instrument. Hold the valves down while pouring the water into the bell. Be sure to rinse with clear warm water. Take a pride in the way your instrument looks by keeping it bright and clean.

FAILURE ON YOUR PART IN NOT FOLLOWING OUT REGULARLY THE ABOVE INSTRUCTIONS, IN REGARD TO THE CARE OF YOUR INSTRUMENT WILL RESULT IN EXPENSIVE REPAIR COSTS.

Table of Harmonics for the Trumpet (Cornet)

Prepared by W. J. Duthoit

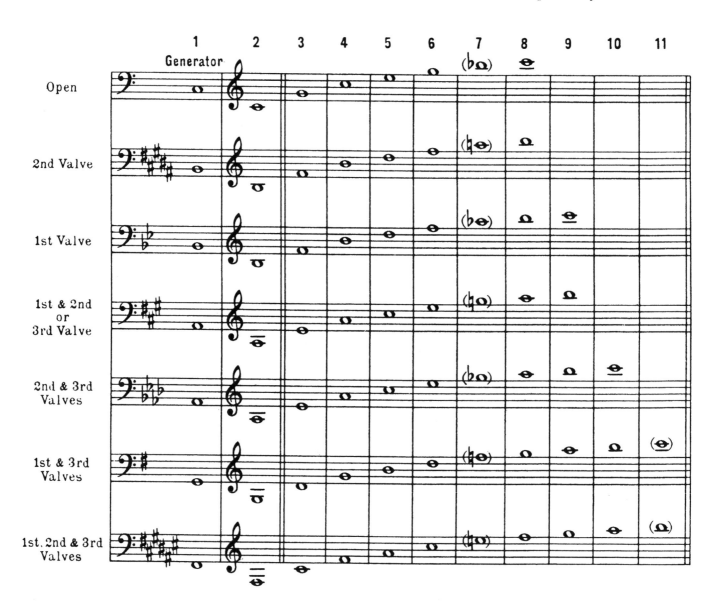

7th Harmonics are flat

11th Harmonics are sharp

[vi]

Reference Fingering Chart
for
Cornet or Trumpet

Correct fingerings for all natural notes within the range of the cornet or trumpet.

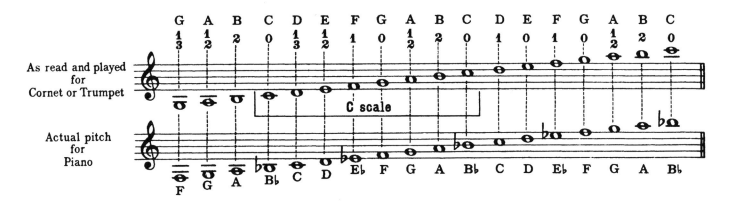

Enharmonic notes: Notes that sound the same, and are fingered the same, but are written differently. Those most frequently used are the following.

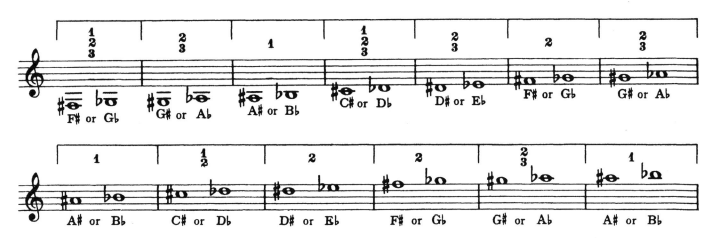

Notice that there are seven combinations of fingering as follows. Notes marked × are playable but slightly out of tune.

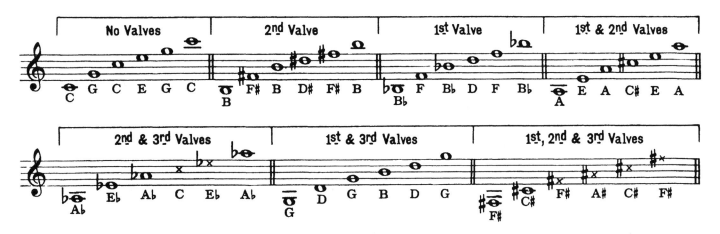

A TUNE A DAY

LESSON 1

OBJECTIVES:
1. To learn the correct habits of
   (a) Holding the trumpet—cornet.
   (b) Position of mouthpiece.
   (c) Breathing and production of tone.
2. To correlate the valves of the cornet with the notes on the staff. G - F
3. To know the value of minims, crotchets and their equivalent rests.
4. To know the meaning of the repeat sign.
5. Answer all questions and do home work.

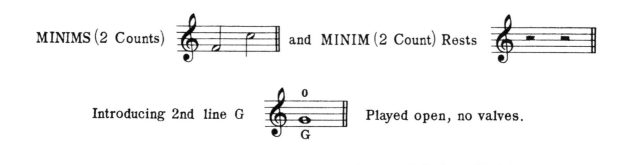

MINIMS (2 Counts) and MINIM (2 Count) Rests

Introducing 2nd line G — Played open, no valves.

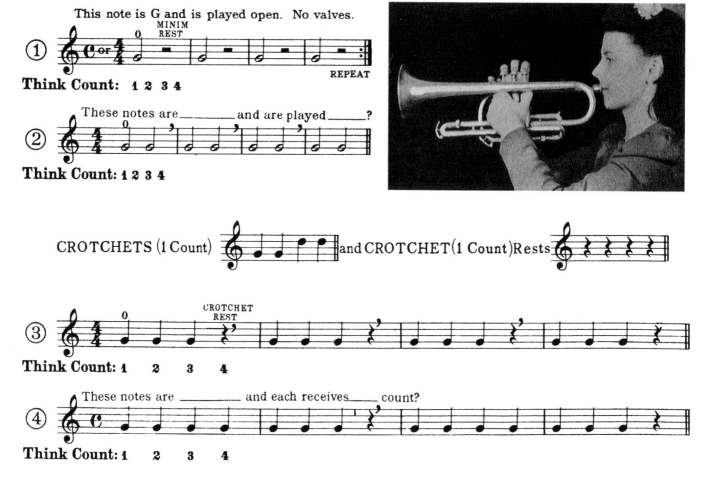

This note is G and is played open. No valves.

① MINIM REST
Think Count: 1 2 3 4

② These notes are _____ and are played _____?
Think Count: 1 2 3 4

CROTCHETS (1 Count) and CROTCHET (1 Count) Rests

③ CROTCHET REST
Think Count: 1 2 3 4

④ These notes are _____ and each receives ____ count?
Think Count: 1 2 3 4

LESSON 1A
Minims and Crotchets

⑤

Think Count: 1 2 3 4   1 2 3 4   1 2 3 4

Introducing 1st space F — Played with the 1st valve.

⑥ This note is F and is played with the 1st valve.

Think Count: 1 2 3 4   REPEAT

⑦ This note is ___ and is played with the ___ valve?

Think Count: 1 2 3 4

⑧ **Think Count:** 1   2   3   4

⑨ These notes are _____ and each receives ___ count?

Think Count: 1   2   3   4

Little F and G March

⑩ This note is ___

Think Count: 1 2 3 4   1 2 3 4

Home work.

Home work: Write a line of crotchets and minims using F and G. Mark the letter name below and the fingering (valves used) above each note.

LESSON 2

OBJECTIVES:
1. Continuation of the objectives of lesson 1.
2. Learning the names and fingerings of the new notes E-D-C.
3. Learn the meaning of the breath mark (᾽)
4. Answer all questions.

Introducing 1st line E.
Played with the 1st & 2nd valves.

Preparation

① This note is E and is played with the 1st & 2nd valves.

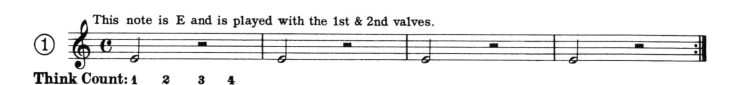

Think Count: 1   2   3   4

② These notes are _____ and each receives_____ counts?

Think Count. 1 2   3 4

③ This note is ___ and is played with the _____ valves?

Think Count: 1   2   3   4

④ These notes are _____ and each receives_____ count?

Think Count: 1   2   3   4

Melody

This note is ___   This note is ___

⑤

Think Count: 1 2   3   4

LESSON 2A

Introducing 1st space below the staff D.
Played with the 1st & 3rd valves.

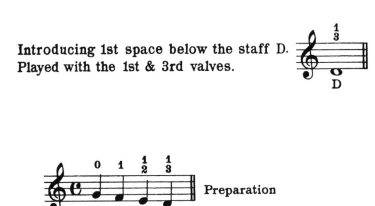

Preparation

This note is D and is played with the 1st & 3rd valves.

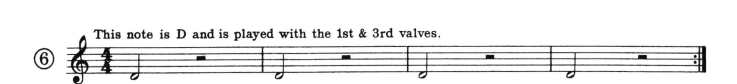

Think Count: 1   2   3   4

These notes are _____ and each receives____ counts?

Think Count: 1 2 3 4

This note is ___ and is played with the _____ valves?

Think Count: 1   2   3   4

These notes are _____ and each receives____ count?

Think Count: 1   2   3   4

Melody

Introducing 1st line below the staff C.
Played open. No valves.

   Preparation

This note is C and is played open. No valves.

⑪

Think Count: 1   2   3   4

These notes are _____ and each receives__ counts?

⑫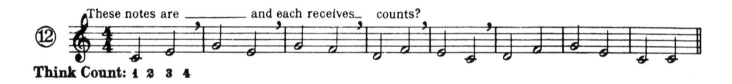

Think Count: 1 2 3 4

This note is ____ and is played _____

⑬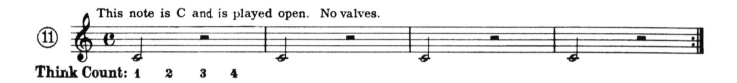

Think Count: 1   2   3   4

These notes are _____ and each receives_____ count?

⑭

Oats and Beans

This note
is ____

⑮

Think Count: 1 2 3 4

LESSON 3

OBJECTIVES: 1. Learn the meaning of the TIE.
2. Application of acquired knowledge in playing familiar melodies.
3. Home work.

Tied Notes

When two notes on the same line or space of the staff are tied by a slur ⁀, they are to be played as one note, adding the value of the two notes together.

Home work: Mark the fingering above, and the letter names below all notes in exercises 3, 4, 5 and 6. Write line of notes thus far studied. Divide into bars using minims and crotchets.

LESSON 4

OBJECTIVES: 1. Learn the value of a semibreve.
2. Comparison of different note values
3. Playing easy duets (both parts).
4. Questions and home work.

These notes are _____ and each receives _____ counts?

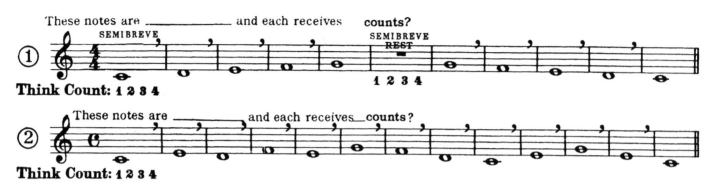

Think Count: 1 2 3 4

These notes are _____ and each receives __ counts?

Think Count: 1 2 3 4

Different Note Values

It is not necessary to play exercise 3 in the order written. Start at the different letters so as to be able to hear and sound any note.

Think Count: 1 2 3 4   1 2 3 4   1 2 3 4   1 2 3 4

Duet (Two Parts)

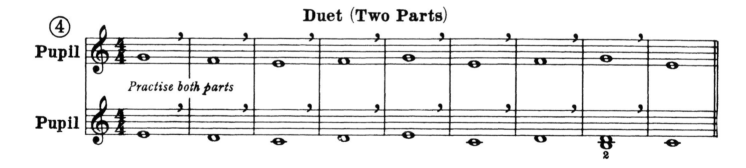

Practise both parts

Trio (Three Parts)

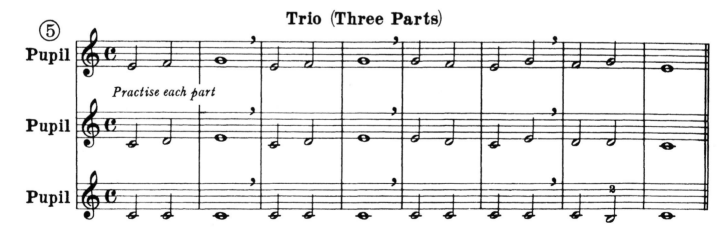

Practise each part

OBJECTIVES:
1. Learning the name and fingering for second space (A).
2. Emphasis on rhythm. (note values)
3. Questions and home work.

Introducing second space A.
Played with the 1st & 2nd valves.

① Think Count: 1 2 3 4

② Think Count: 1 2 3 4

③

④ **Little G and A March**

Think Count: 1 2 3 4

⑤ **Melody**

Think Count: 1 2 3 4

⑥ **Folk Song**

Think Count: 1 2 3 4

⑦ **Twinkle, Twinkle, Little Star**

Think Count: 1 2 3 4

The Boat Song

Unfamiliar Melody—Test
Think fingering and note values.

C. P. H.

MINIM REST

⑧ Think Count: 1 2 3 4

Home work: You can't be too familiar with the names of notes and their fingerings so if you wish to learn, mark this lesson as before.

TEST QUESTIONS ON LESSONS 1-5

Questions from this, and following test-sheets, will be given as a check on your home-study of preceding lessons.

REMEMBER: The more you know and understand about the signs and symbols used in music-writing, the easier it will be for you to learn how to play well.

	Points.	Your score
(1) This ▤ is called? _____	4	....
(2) This symbol 𝄞 is called? _____	4	....
(3) The **staff** is divided by bar-lines into? _____	4	....
(4) Fractions at the beginning of music are called _____ signatures?	4	....
(5) This 𝄞 𝅝 is a _____ and has _____ counts?	4	....
(6) These 𝄞 𝅗𝅥 𝅗𝅥 are _____ and have _____ counts each?	4	....
(7) These 𝄞 ♩ ♩ ♩ ♩ are _____ and have _____ count each?	4	....
(8) Lines and spaces are named after the first _____ letters of the alphabet?	4	....
(9) This 𝄞 𝄻 is a _____ rest?	4	....
(10) These 𝄞 𝄼 𝄼 are _____ rests?	4	....
(11) These 𝄞 𝄾 𝄾 𝄾 𝄾 are _____ rests?	4	....
(12) This 𝄞 (C or 4/4) means _____ to each bar?	4	....
(13) Name the notes thus far studied _____	6	....
(14) Write the notes thus far studied. 𝄞	6	....
(15) Write the letter names below and the fingering above the following notes.	10	....

(16) Inspection of instrument*   10 ....

(17) Sight reading test   20 ....

            100

TEACHER: Write line of notes thus far studied, using semibreves, crotchets and quavers as a sight-reading test

*This inspection should be followed up at each test period.

Supplementary Material for Lessons 1-2-3-4 & 5

Theme from Good King Wenceslas

Crusaders' Hymn

Long, Long Ago

Bayly

Melody

God Save The Queen*

* Although neither three-four time, nor B♮ have been introduced up to lesson 5, this familiar melody is given here as a challenge to the student.

LESSON 6

OBJECTIVES: 1. Learning the meaning of the ♯, and the ♮.
2. Learning the name and fingering for 1st space F♯.
3. Learn the meaning of an accidental.
4. Application of acquired knowledge in playing familiar melodies.

Introducing first space F sharp (F♯)
Played with the 2nd valve

A SHARP (♯) RAISES THE NOTE TO WHICH IT APPLIES BY A SEMITONE.

A NATURAL (♮) TAKES AWAY THE EFFECT OF A SHARP OR FLAT.

① Think Count: 1 2 3 4

② Think Count: 1 2 3 4

③ Think Count: 1 2 3 4

NOTICE THE F♯ AT THE BEGINNING OF PIECES 4 AND 5. THAT MEANS THAT EVERY F THROUGHOUT THE PIECE WILL BE PLAYED SHARP. (SECOND VALVE)

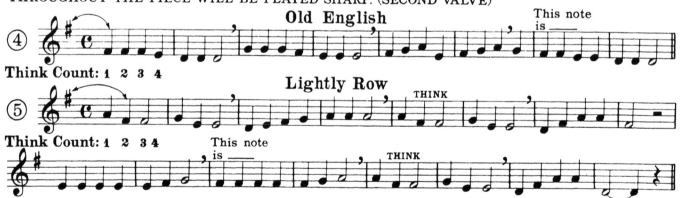

Old English

④ Think Count: 1 2 3 4   This note is _____

Lightly Row

⑤ Think Count: 1 2 3 4   THINK

This note is _____   THINK

ALWAYS NOTICE THE SHARPS OR FLATS AT THE BEGINNING OF THE LINE AND THINK WHAT THEY MEAN BEFORE PLAYING ANY EXERCISE OR PIECE.

AN ACCIDENTAL IS A SHARP OR FLAT WHICH DOES NOT BELONG TO THE KEY SIGNATURE. SEE SEVENTH BAR EX. 6, THE F♯

NO SHARP   Think fingering and note values   **Hymn**   Monk   THINK   REST

⑥

This note is _____

Home work: **Mark the fingering above, and the name below all notes in Ex. 4, 5 and 6.**

LESSON 7

OBJECTIVES:
1. Learn the meaning of key signatures.
2. Learn the key of D major (F♯ and C♯), of C major,(no sharps or flats).
3. Application of acquired knowledge in playing DUETS.
4. Learning to hear intervals (difference in pitch between two notes).

Key Signatures

The Sharps or Flats found after the Clef at the beginning of each line is called the Key Signature. These Sharps or Flats affect all the notes of the same name throughout the piece, except when changed by a new Key signature or temporarily by an accidental.

THE KEY OF C HAS NO SHARPS OR FLATS. EX.1 and 4. THE KEY OF D HAS 2 SHARPS, (F♯ and C♯). EX. 2 and 3. ALWAYS THINK THE SHARPS OR FLATS AS INDICATED IN THE KEY SIGNATURE and finger the notes accordingly.

Duets (Practise Both Parts)

Upidee (Key of C — No sharps (♯) or flats (♭)

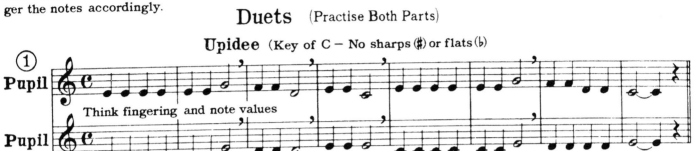

Upidee (Key of D— Two sharps (F♯ & C♯)

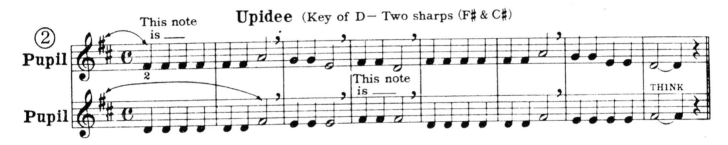

Merrily (Key of ____ the sharps are _____)

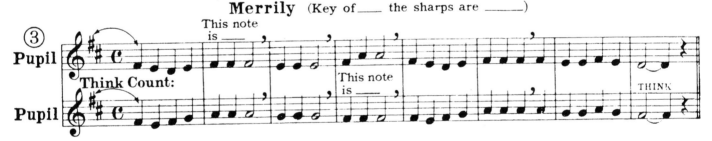

Au clair de la lune (Key of ____)

LESSON 8

OBJECTIVES: 1. Learning the name and fingering for third line B flat.
2. Learn the meaning of a flat (♭).
3. Learning the proper use of the lip muscles to produce the higher notes.
4. Learning the key of F. One flat (B♭)
5. To recognize and know the meaning of the up beat.

Introducing third line B♭
Played with the 1st valve

A FLAT(♭) LOWERS THE NOTE TO WHICH IT APPLIES BY A SEMITONE

BEFORE NAMING OR PLAYING ANY NOTE BE SURE TO NOTICE THE KEY SIGNATURE.

Key of F, one flat (♭). The flat (♭) placed on the third line of the staff, just after the clef sign, means to flat every B, except where cancelled by a natural (♮).

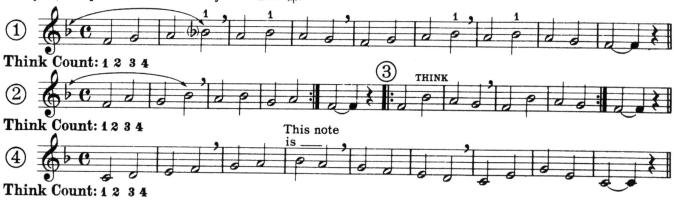

Many pieces begin with an incomplete bar, usually starting with the last beat or fraction thereof. This is called the up-beat. The ending always completes the bar of the up-beat.

An accidental is a sharp or flat which does not belong to the key signature. An accidental applies only to the bar in which it is placed. Ex. 5, F♯.

Home work: Write line of notes thus far studied, using semibreves, minims and crotchets. Mark **fingering above** and letter names below.

LESSON 9

OBJECTIVES:
1. Learning the name and fingering for third line B (natural)
2. Continual emphasis on rhythm and fingering
3. Learning the key of G (one sharp F♯)

Introducing third line B♮
Played with the 2nd valve
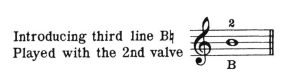

Think Count: 1 2 3 4

Think Count: 1 2 3 4

Melody

Think Count: 1 2 3 4

KEY OF G—ONE SHARP. THE SHARP IS F♯. MEANS TO SHARP EVERY F UNLESS CANCELLED BY A NATURAL SIGN (♮).

Folk Song

Key of ____ The sharp is ____ Time sig. is ____

Think Count: 1 2 3 4

Folk Song

Key of ____ Sharps are ____

Think fingering and note values

Sight reading *

* *Teacher:* Write line of notes used through this lesson as a sight reading test.
Use key signature and accidentals.

Supplementary Material for Lessons 6-7-8 & 9

Integer Vitae

Melody

Twinkle, Twinkle, Little Star

Harvest Time

OBJECTIVES:
1. Learning the name and fingering for third space C.
2. To know the formation of the natural scale, (Placement of whole tones and semitones).
3. Playing the C scale and arpeggio from memory. (Ex. 8 and 9)
4. Slurring notes in groups of two and four.

Introducing third space C
Played open (no valves)

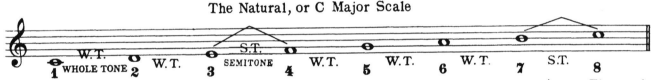

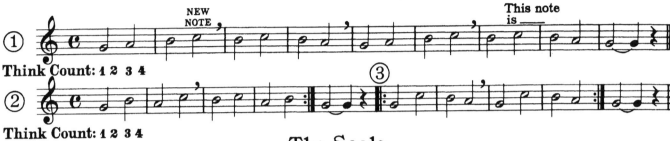

The Scale

A scale is a progression from a given note (key note) to its octave, 8 notes higher. The form on which all major scales are modelled is as follows:

The Natural, or C Major Scale

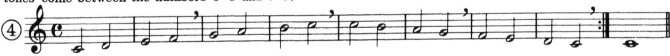

The ascending progression is: two whole tones, one semitone, three whole tones, one semitone. The semitones come between the numbers 3-4 and 7-8.

Slurred Notes (*legato)

This sign (⌢ slur) when placed above or below two or more notes indicates that they are to be connected. TONGUE ONLY THE FIRST NOTE OF ANY GROUP OF SLURRED NOTES.

* Smoothly- connected.   **Play also slurring four notes.
Home work: Learn to recite and play the C major scale from memory.

TEST QUESTIONS ON LESSONS 6-10

		Points	Your score

(1) This sign :||: means? _____   2   ....

(2) This ♯ is a? _____   2   ....

(3) How does a ♯ affect a note? _____   4   ....

(4) This ♮ is a? _____   2   ....

(5) How does a ♮ affect a note? _____   4   ....

(6) Name the following lines and spaces of the staff?   8   ....

      1st space _____   2nd space _____
      3rd space _____   1st line _____
      3rd line _____   2nd line _____
      1st line below staff _____   1st space below staff _____

(7) This ♭ is a? _____   2   ....

(8) How does a ♭ affect a note? _____   4   ....

(9) What is an accidental? _____   4   ....

(10) The key of 2♯ is? _____   4   ....

(11) Write the key signature of 2♯   4   ....

(12) What notes are played with the following valves?   9   ....

      1st valve _____ and _____   1st & 2nd valves _____ and _____
      No valves _____ and _____   1st & 3rd valves _____
               2nd valve _____ and _____

(13) Write the notes in question 12 in the order given?   9   ....

(14) This sign ⌢ connecting two or more notes means? _____   2   ....

(15) What is a scale? _____   5   ....

(16) Write the C major scale?   7   ....

(17) The key of 1♭ is? _____   2   ....

(18) The key of 1♯ is? _____   2   ....

(19) Write the key signatures of 1♭ and 1♯?   4   ....

(20) Sight reading   20   ....
                          100

TEACHER: Write line of notes thus far studied, using semibreves, minims and crotchets. Use slurs.

LESSON 11

OBJECTIVES
1. The use of slurred notes in familiar melodies.
2. Rhythms involving quavers in 4/4 and 2/4 time.
3. Correlation of notes thus far studied (name and position on the staff) with proper fingering.

Hymn
J. Hatton

Observe slurs carefully

Lightly Row

Observe slurs carefully

Quavers

A quaver is equal to ½ of a crotchet, and receives ½ of a count in 4/4 or 2/4 time. Two quavers equal one crotchet, or one count, four quavers equal one minim (2 counts) and eight quavers equal one semibreve (4 counts)

BE SURE TO LEARN THE RHYTHM DRILLS THOROUGHLY (learn to feel the division of the beats) BEFORE PLAYING THE MELODIES. THIS IS IMPORTANT.

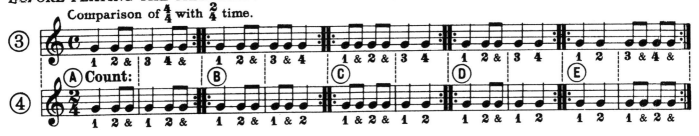

Old English Song

Gaily The Troubadour

Home work: Write line of notes thus far studied, using minims, crotchets and quavers in 2/4 time.

Supplementary Material for Lessons 10 & 11

Evening Song

OBJECTIVES: 1. Learning new rhythm — $\frac{3}{4}$ time — with emphasis
on rhythm drills. (A - B - C etc.)
2. Use of dotted crotchets and quavers. (Ex. F)
3. The application of acquired knowledge

The Dotted Minim and the Dotted Crotchet

A dot is equal to one half the value of the note it follows. A dotted minim equals 3 beats, a dotted crotchet equals $1\frac{1}{2}$ beats.

Rhythm Drills

DRILL: Count aloud each variation, A-B-C etc. while clapping the hands once for each note until the rhythms are felt and memorized, then try to play them using any single note. When this can be done freely, play the exercises as written. REMEMBER — Rhythm must be felt before it can be played.

Combination of Rhythms in 3/4 time

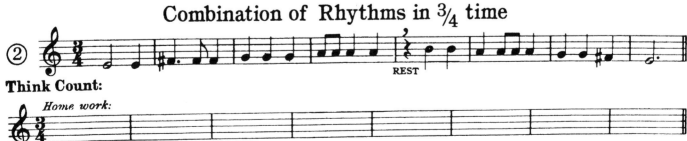

Think Count:

Home work:

Home work: Write 8 bars of notes thus far studied, using different groupings of notes in $\frac{3}{4}$ time. Mark fingering and note names as before.

LESSON 13

[Continuation of Dotted Minims and Dotted Crotchets in $\frac{3}{4}$ and $\frac{2}{2}$ Time]

OBJECTIVES:
1. Application of $\frac{3}{4}$ and $\frac{2}{4}$ rhythms in familiar melodies of different keys.
2. Knowledge of the first- and second- time bars.
3. Learning to play melodies from memory.
4. Application of slurs and key changes.
5. Knowledge of terms used for tempo (speed)

First- and Second-Time Bars

The term 1st and 2nd time bars applies to one or more bars in brackets at a double bar; thus when the strain is repeated, the first time bar is omitted and the second time bar played instead.

Home work: Learn to play one of the above melodies from memory.

LESSON 14

OBJECTIVES: 1. Application of previously acquired knowledge.
2. Carols for recreation.
3. Knowledge of the fermata ⌢ (pause)

We Three Kings of Orient Are

Moderate speed (Moderato)

Key of _____ The flat is _____ Time sig. is _____

Hopkins

Think Count: 1 2 3

O Come, All Ye Faithful
Adeste Fidelis

Moderato

Key of _____ The flat is _____ Time sig. is _____

XIII Century Latin Hymn

Think Count: 4   1 2 3   4

Deck the Halls

Brightly (Allegretto)

Key of _____ Time sig. is _____

Think Count: 1 2 & 3   4

* ⌢ Pause (fermata) A short curved line drawn over a dot, prolongs the time of the note.
Home work: Learn to play from memory the above melodies.

LESSON 15

OBJECTIVES: 1. Learning the name and fingering of fourth line D.
2. Memorizing the National Anthem.
3. Application of acquired knowledge in varied keys and rhythms.

Introducing fourth line D   Played with the 1st valve

Home work: Write line of notes thus far studied, using different note values. Mark valves used above and name below.

Supplementary Material for Lessons 12-13-14 & 15
Stephen Foster Melodies

Old Folks at Home

Massa's in the Cold, Cold Ground

My Old Kentucky Home

Oh! Susanna

TEST QUESTIONS ON LESSONS 11-15

		Points	Your score

(1) These [music notation] are _____ ? — 5 ········

(2) Each of the above notes receives _____ count? — 5 ········

(3) This [music notation] is a _____ ? — 5 ········

(4) The above note has _____ counts? — 5 ········

(5) This [music notation] is a _____ ? — 5 ········

(6) The above note has _____ counts? — 5 ········

(7) Divide the following into bars? — 5 ········

[music notation]

(8) Mark the count under the following? — 5 ········

[music notation]

(9) This [music notation] means? _____ — 5 ········

(10) This sign ⌒ means? _____ — 5 ········

(11) What is meant by the up beat? _____ — 5 ········

(12) Music written for two cornets is called a? _____ — 5 ········

(13) How many notes can you play with each of the following valves? — 10 ········

No valves ____   1st valve ____   2nd valve ____   1st & 2nd valves ____

(14) Write (notate) your answers to question 13 in the order given? — 10 ········

[music staff]

(15) Sight reading — 20 ········
  — — 100

[music staff]

TEACHER: Write line of notes using different rhythm patterns in $\frac{3}{4}$ time.

LESSON 16

OBJECTIVES:
1. Learning the name and fingering for low B♮.
2. Learning the proper use of the lip muscles to produce the lower notes.
3. Knowledge of key and rhythm changes.
4. The playing of quavers in a faster tempo. (Ex. 5)
5. The playing of two quavers on the up-beat. (Ex. 4)

Introducing low B♮   Played with the 2nd valve

Think Count: 1 2 3 4

Melody

Think Count: 1 2 3 4

Folk Song

Think Count: 1 2 3 4

Folk Song

Think Count: 3 & 1 2 3

Little Brown Jug

Think Count: & 1 & 2 &

Waltz Theme

C.P.H.

Tempo di Valse

Think Count 1 2 3 1 2 3

Home work:

Home work: Write line of notes in $\frac{2}{4}$, using new note in this lesson and mark as before, also write line in $\frac{3}{4}$. Use different valued notes thus far studied.

28

LESSON 17
(Duets)

OBJECTIVES:
1. Ability to play independent secondary parts where the note values are not the same as in the first part.
2. Application of acquired knowledge of slurs and accidentals.

American Hymn

Keller

OBJECTIVES: 1. Learning the name and fingering for fourth space E.
2. Application of proper use of lip muscles to
produce higher notes.
3. Application of all subject-matter learned thus far.

Introducing fourth space E   Played open

Home work: Write line of notes, using the new note in this lesson. Mark fingering and note names as before.
Mark exercise 4 the same way.

Supplementary Material for Lessons 16-17 & 18

(LIP SLURS)

OBJECTIVE: Application of proper use of lip muscles
to play lip slurs.

The material in this lesson is to be used whenever necessary according to the teacher's directions.

Repeat the above bugle call using the different valve combinations below.

Army bugle calls are written on four notes and may be played with any of the following valve combinations

LESSON 19

OBJECTIVES:
1. Learning the name and fingering for low Bb.
2. Knowledge of the key of Bb (Bb & Eb)
3. Application of acquired knowledge through the playing of familiar and unfamiliar melodies.
4. Learn fingering of low A. (Ex. 6, lower part)

Introducing low Bb — Played with the 1st valve

Key of Bb, 2 flats, Bb & Eb. These flats, placed at the beginning of each staff, mean flatten every B & E, except when cancelled by a natural (♮).

Merrily

Familiar Melodies *(Listen carefully)*

French Folk Song

Harvest Time

Andante (Slowly)
Unfamiliar Melody– Test

C.P.H.

Duet

von Weber

Andante (Slowly)

LESSON 20
(Intermediate notes— Chromatics)

OBJECTIVES:
1. Understanding and playing chromatics
2. Knowledge of enharmonic notes.
3. Learning new fingerings.

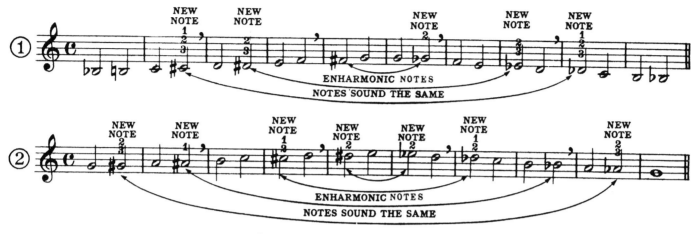

Chromatic Scales

The word "chromatic" means moving by semitones. A chromatic scale is one that ascends or descends by half steps.

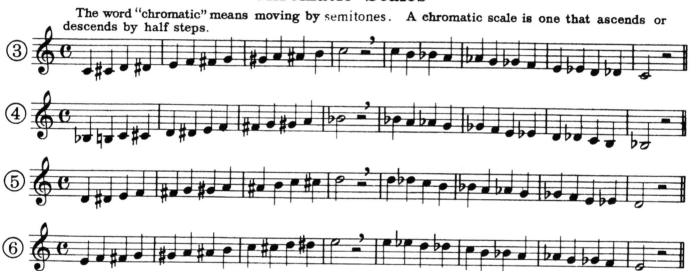

IF YOU CAN'T SPELL A WORD YOU CAN'T WRITE IT. IF YOU CAN'T SPELL (RECITE) A SCALE YOU CAN'T PLAY IT. LEARN TO RECITE ALL SCALES BEFORE PLAYING.

Scale of B♭ (Two flats)

The flats are ___ and ___

Scale of D (Two sharps)

The sharps are ___ and ___

Scale of E♭ (Three flats)

The flats are ___, ___ and ___

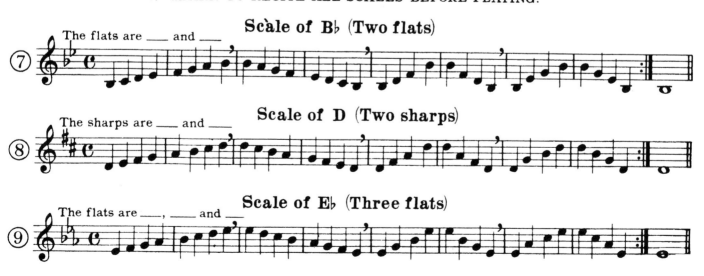

TEST QUESTIONS ON LESSONS 16-20

	Points	Your score

(1) The letter name of this note [musical note] is? _____   2   ....

(2) The above note is played with _____ valves?   3   ....

(3) The name of this note [musical note] is? _____   2   ....

(4) The above note is played with the _____ valve?   3   ....

(5) The key of two flats (♭) is? _____   2   ....

(6) The flats are? ___ and ___   3   ....

(7) What is meant by enharmonic notes? _____   5   ....

(8) Write the enharmonic equivalents of the following notes?   5   ....

[musical staff with notes]

(9) What is meant by chromatics? _____   5   ....

(10) Write the scale of B♭ major?   10   ....

[blank musical staff]

(11) Write the scale of D major?   10   ....

[blank musical staff]

(12) Write the scale of E♭ major?   10   ....

[blank musical staff]

(13) Play one of the above scales from memory?   10   ....

(14) Write letter name above and fingering below the following notes?   10   ....

[musical staff with notes]

(15) Sight reading   20   ....
                      100

[blank musical staff]

TEACHER: Write line of notes using chromatics.

Melodies in the Keys of D - B♭ & E♭

Cradle Song

Andante (Slowly)

Brahms

Key of ⎯⎯ Sharps are ⎯⎯⎯

Recite and play scale of this key

Believe Me If All Those Endearing Young Charms

Allegretto (Brightly)

Irish Melody

Key of ⎯⎯ Flats are ⎯⎯⎯

Home, Sweet Home

Andante (Slowly)

Henry R. Bishop

Key of ⎯⎯ Flats are ⎯⎯⎯

Recite and play scale of this key

THINK

Home work: Play from memory the scales of the keys used in this lesson.

LESSON 22

OBJECTIVES: 1.   Learning a new rhythm.
2.   Understanding Alla breve (cut time) ($\frac{2}{2}$ time)

Comparison of ¢ with $\frac{2}{4}$ time

Rhythm Drills

Drill: Count aloud each pattern while clapping the hands once for each note.
REMEMBER – Unless you feel a rhythm you cannot play it.
Play the C scale, using these patterns until the rhythms are memorized.

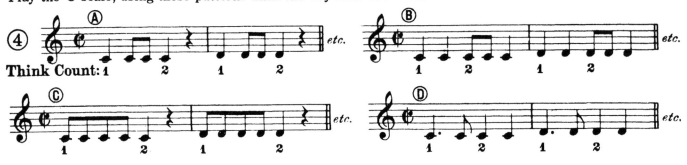

There's Music in the Air

Root

Key of ___ Sharp is ___ Time sig. is ___

Think Count: &   1 & 2 &

LESSON 23

OBJECTIVES: 1. Continuation of Alla breve (cut time).
2. The playing of a full length march.
3. Application of acquired knowledge.
4. Knowledge of the meaning of this sign (⁒).
5. Knowledge of signs indicating volume of tone (dynamics).

Advancement March*

In March time (Not too fast)   C. P. H.

* All marches generally consist of an introduction, 1st and 2nd strain, each repeated, followed by a Trio. The key of the Trio is always a fifth lower than that of the first part.
**This sign ⁒ means to repeat the preceding bar.

LESSON 24

OBJECTIVES:
1. Learning another new rhythm.
2. Knowledge and use of the rhythm of $\frac{6}{8}$ time.
3. Counting 6 to a bar and 2 to a bar.
4. Application of new rhythm in familiar melodies.

Row, Row, Row Your Boat

Oats and Beans

Mulberry Bush

Home work: Write line of notes, using different rhythm patterns in $\frac{6}{8}$ time.

LESSON 25

OBJECTIVES:
1. Continuation of six-eight time. (slow)
2. Counting six beats to a bar.
3. Application of acquired knowledge in familiar tunes.
4. Playing of duet in six-eight time.

It Came Upon a Midnight Clear

* *rit.,* abbreviation of *ritenuto* — gradually slower in speed.

	Points	Your score

(1) This sign ₵ means? _____   4   ....

(2) A minim receives _____ count in cut time?   4   ....

(3) Divide the following into bars?   5   ....

(4) What is meant by six-eight ($\frac{6}{8}$ time)?   4   ....

(5) This note   has _____ counts?   4   ....

(6) This note   has _____ counts?   4   ....

(7) Mark the count under the following?   5   ....

(8) Divide the following into bars?   5   ....

(9) What notes are played, from low to high, with the following valves?   12   ....

1st valve   1 ___ 2 ___ 3 ___ 4 ___   2nd & 3rd valves   1 ___   2 ___

2nd valve   1 ___   2 ___   3 ___   1st & 2nd valves   1 ___   2 ___   8 ___

(10) Write your answers to question 9?   12   ....

(11) In $\frac{6}{8}$ march tempo (fast) the count is _____ beats to each bar?   4   ....

(12) In $\frac{6}{8}$ slow tempo the count is _____ beats to a bar?   4   ....

(13) This sign ⁒. means? _____   3   ....

(14) Notate the key signatures of G - F - B♭ - D - E♭?   10   ....

(15) Sight reading   20   ....

                        100

TEACHER: Write line of notes in slow six-eight time in the key of B♭.

LESSON 26

OBJECTIVES:
1. Continuation of six-eight time. (fast)
2. Counting **two beats to a** bar. (march time)
3. Application of acquired knowledge in familiar tunes.
4. Playing of march in six-eight time.

Skipping Along
(Duet)

C.P.H.

* Accent ＞

LESSON 27

OBJECTIVES: Learning the use of semiquavers.
           (a) Equivalents
           (b) Counting semiquavers.

Semiquavers

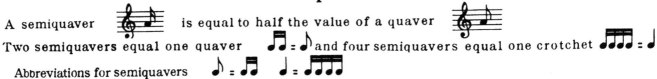

A semiquaver is equal to half the value of a quaver

Two semiquavers equal one quaver and four semiquavers equal one crotchet

Abbreviations for semiquavers

Comparative table showing number of semiquavers to other notes studied thus far.

① Note time signatures

② Note time signatures

④

③ Note time signatures

Mac Donald's Farm

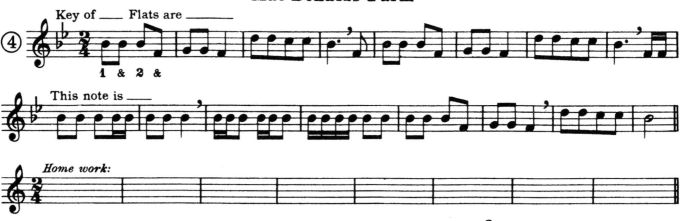

④ Key of ___ Flats are ___

This note is ___

Home work:

Home work: Write line of notes, using different groupings of semiquavers in $\frac{2}{4}$ time.
           Memorize "Reveille" on page 31 exercise 4.

LESSON 28

43

OBJECTIVES: 1. **Dotted** quavers and semiquavers, legato
  2. **Correct division of each beat.**
  3. **Application of new rhythm.**

Dotted Quavers and Semiquavers
Legato (Connected)

This is one of the more difficult rhythms to learn. The dotted quaver is equal to three semiquavers. Always feel a division of four on each beat when playing this rhythm, three on the dotted quaver and one on

the semiquaver.

BE SURE TO PLAY THE DOTTED QUAVER LONG ENOUGH AND THE SEMIQUAVER SHORT ENOUGH.

Home work: Write line of notes, using dotted quavers and semiquavers.
    * *cresc.* — Gradually louder.

LESSON 29

OBJECTIVES:
1. Dotted quavers and semiquavers staccato. (detached)
2. Application of this difficult rhythm in familiar melodies using $\frac{2}{4}$ and $\frac{4}{4}$ time.

Dotted Quavers and Semiquavers
Staccato (Detached)

Dotted quavers and semiquavers played staccato (detached) are separated by a short pause as follows:

Joy to the World
(Duet)

Handel

Home work: Memorise "Assembly" and "Call to the Colours" on page 31

LESSON 30

OBJECTIVE: Continued application of dotted quavers and semiquavers in $\frac{3}{4}$ and $\frac{6}{8}$ time.

Maryland, My Maryland
(Duet)

Silent Night, Holy Night
(Duet)

Gruber

LESSON 31

OBJECTIVES:
1. Learning the name and fingering for top line F.
2. Playing the scale of F major from memory.
3. Using new notes in familiar melodies.

Introducing top line F♮   Played with the 1st valve

Scale and Arpeggio of F Major

The flat is ___ Recite scale before playing

Con moto (With motion)   **The First Noël**

Key of ___ Flat is ___

Introducing top line F♯   Played with the 2nd valve

Allegretto   **America, the Beautiful**   Ward

Key of ___ Sharps are ___

This note is ___

Moderato   **The Blacksmith**   Mozart

Key of ___ Sharps are ___

Home work:

Home work: Write the F major scale. Use key signature and place flats before the notes affected. Learn to play F major scale from memory.

OBJECTIVES:
1. Learning the name and fingering for high G.
2. Playing the scale of G major from memory.
3. Learning variations to Ex. 5.

Introducing high G   Played open

The sharp is ____ Recite scale before playing

Scale Study

Key of ____

Practise the following variations of tongueing on Ex. (5)

Old Russian Hymn

Lento (Slowly)

Key of ____ Sharp is ____

Pupil   *mf*

Practise both parts

Pupil   *mf*

cresc.   *f*   *dim.*

Home work:

Home work: Write the G major scale. Use key signature and place sharp before the notes affected. Learn to play G major scale from memory.

TEST QUESTIONS ON LESSONS 26-32

	Points	Your score

(1) These [music notation] are _____ ?   4   ....

(2) Four (4) of the above notes equal a _____ ?   4   ....

(3) Divide the following into bars?   5   ....

[music notation]

(4) This 7 is a _____ rest?   3   ....

(5) Circle the notes in the following line that begin each beat?   5   ....

[music notation]

(6) A [dotted quaver] is equal to _____ semiquavers?   4   ....

(7) A [minim] is equal to _____ semiquavers?   4   ....

(8) This [music notation] is equal to a _____ note?   4   ....

(9) Write five (5) bars, using dotted-quavers and semiquavers?   5   ....

[music staff]

(10) Divide the following into bars?   5   ....

[music notation]

(11) This note [music notation] is _____ and is played with the _____ valve?   4   ....

(12) Write the scale of the key of one flat?   5   ....

[music staff]

(13) This note [music notation] is _____ and is played with the _____ valve?   4   ....

(14) This note [music notation] is _____ and is played with _____ valves?   4   ....

(15) Play the scale of F major from memory?   5   ....

(16) Write the letter-names of the G major scale? _____   5   ....

(17) Write the key signatures of D - F - G - B♭ - E♭?   10   ....

[music staves]

(18) Sight reading   20
                       ———
                       100   ....

[music staff]

TEACHER: Write line of notes using dotted-quavers and semiquavers, slurs, accidentals etc.

Six Trios

Onward, Christian Soldiers
Trio

Sir Arthur Sullivan

Vesper Hymn
(Trio)

Deck the Hall
(Trio)

Theme From "Lobgesang"
(Trio)

Mendelssohn

Con moto (With motion)

Pupil

Pupil

Pupil

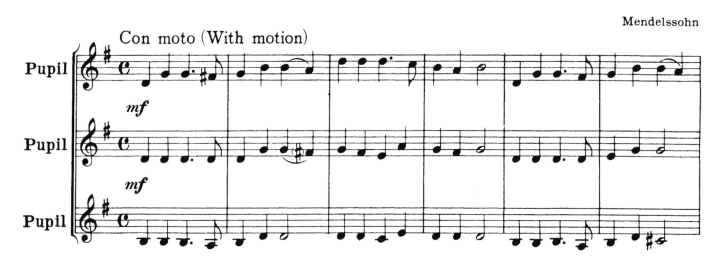

O Little Town of Bethlehem
(Trio)

Silent Night, Holy Night
(Trio)

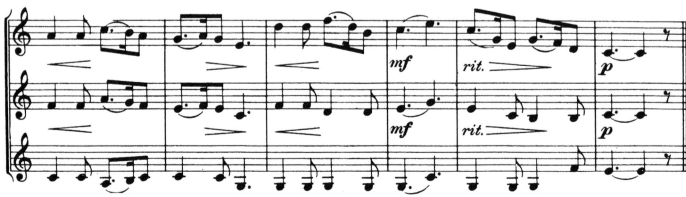

Printed by Printwise (Haverhill) Limited, Suffolk   10/08 (167337)